C. P. CAVAFY

SELECTED POEMS

C. P. CAVAFY

SELECTED POEMS

Translated by

Edmund Keeley and Philip Sherrard

PRINCETON UNIVERSITY PRESS

PRINCETON, NEW JERSEY

L.C. Card: 70-39789
Clothbound *ISBN: 0-691-06228-5*
Paperback *ISBN: 0-691-01304-1*
This book has been set in Linotype Monticello

The Greek texts of the following poems are
copyright © 1968 by Kiveli A. Singopoulou:

Growing in Spirit
Antony's Ending
Returning from Greece
Exiles
Half an Hour

Printed in the United States of America
by Princeton University Press,
Princeton, New Jersey

Foreword

THIS selected volume of Cavafy was prompted by our realization, while preparing a forthcoming complete bilingual edition of the Greek poet's mature work, that there was need at this time for a new English version of his most significant and characteristic poems. What we offer here reflects our estimate of the best of Cavafy and our latest efforts as translators to do adequate justice to his voice. Though this selection obviously excludes a number of poems Cavafy himself considered worthy of collection, we have tried to include all of those poems that are now generally accepted as his main contribution to poetry in this century. We have also tried to include poems representative of his major themes and modes, without giving undue emphasis to any one of these.

Our realization of the need for new versions of poems already available to the English reader arose out of a growing sense that Cavafy should be rendered in a style that is neither stilted nor artificial. Cavafy's use of language— a carefully modulated synthesis of *katharevousa* and *demotiki*—easily lends itself to mistranslation. It has become increasingly clear to us, during our work on Cavafy's poetry over the past twenty years, that his voice is more natural, immediate, and even colloquial than extant translations— including our own earlier selections—would make it appear. Cavafy's Greek, even with its deliberate archaisms, is closer in crucial ways to the spoken idiom than is the language of other leading Greek poets of his time. It is this idiom that we hope is reflected in the language and rhythm we have chosen to use in these new versions. It seemed to us especially important to avoid any artificiality or pedantic literalness in poems that are predominantly dramatic. We have therefore made no attempt to reproduce Cavafy's sporadic rhyme schemes and syntactical idiosyncrasies, though we have tried to create a style as natural and apt in English as his generally is in Greek.

E. K.
P. S.
Katounia, Limni,
Euboea, 1971

Acknowledgments

WE are grateful to Mrs. Kyvelli Singopoulou for granting us permission to include five poems from the volume of unpublished poems, Ἀνέκδοτα Ποιήματα, *1882-1923*, which appeared in Athens in 1968 (Ikaros). We are also grateful to the editor of the volume, Mr. George Savidis, for his collaboration in the first English versions of these poems, published in *C. P. Cavafy: Passions and Ancient Days* (The Dial Press, New York, 1971). Zisimos Lorentzatos offered a number of valuable suggestions regarding the translation. The details in the Biographical Note (p. 91) are based in large part on data generously supplied by Stratis Tsirkas, author of Ὁ Καβάφης καὶ ἡ Ἐποχή του (Kedros, Athens, 1958). Mr. Tsirkas indicates the unpublished notes of Rika Singopoulou-Agallianou as one of his sources.

Translations from this volume have appeared in *The New Yorker*, *The New York Review of Books*, *Quarterly Review of Literature*, *Antaeus*, *New Letters*, *Boundary 2*, *Shenandoah*, and *Poetry* ("The Footsteps," "The Ides of March," "Theodotos"), copyright © Modern Poetry Association, 1972.

Other Books by the Translators

Edmund Keeley

THE LIBATION

SIX POETS OF MODERN GREECE, *with Philip Sherrard*

THE GOLD-HATTED LOVER

VASSILIS VASSILIKOS: THE PLANT, THE WELL, THE
ANGEL, *with Mary Keeley*

GEORGE SEFERIS: COLLECTED POEMS, 1924-1955, *with
Philip Sherrard*

THE IMPOSTOR

C. P. CAVAFY: PASSIONS AND ANCIENT DAYS, *with George
Savidis*

MODERN GREEK WRITERS, *Editor, with Peter Bien*

VOYAGE TO A DARK ISLAND

Philip Sherrard

THE MARBLE THRESHING FLOOR

THE GREEK EAST AND THE LATIN WEST

ATHOS, THE MOUNTAIN OF SILENCE

SIX POETS OF MODERN GREECE, *with Edmund Keeley*

THE PURSUIT OF GREECE, *Editor*

CONSTANTINOPLE: ICONOGRAPHY OF A SACRED CITY

BYZANTIUM

GEORGE SEFERIS: COLLECTED POEMS, 1924-1955, *with
Edmund Keeley*

MODERN GREECE, *with John Campbell*

Contents

C. P. CAVAFY

SELECTED POEMS

The poems in this selection are arranged
in chronological order, the first dated 1901
and the last 1933. An asterisk by the title
indicates that a note to the poem appears
under Notes, beginning on page 85.

For some people there's a day
when they have to come out with the great Yes
or the great No. It's clear at once
who has the Yes ready in him; and saying it,

he goes on to find honor, strong in his conviction.
He who refuses never repents. Asked again,
he'd still say no. Yet that no—the right answer—
defeats him the whole of his life.

Honor to those who in the life they lead
define and guard a Thermopylae.
Never betraying what is right,
consistent and just in all they do
but showing pity also, and compassion;
generous when they're rich, and when they're poor,
still generous in small ways,
still helping whenever they can;
always speaking the truth
yet without hating those who lie.

And even more honor is due to them
when they foresee (as many do foresee)
that Ephialtis will turn up in the end,
that the Medes will break through after all.

He who hopes to grow in spirit
will have to free himself from obedience and respect.
He'll hold to some laws
but he'll mostly violate
both law and custom, and go beyond
the established, inadequate norm.
Sexual pleasure will have much to teach him.
He won't be afraid of the destructive act:
half the house will have to come down.
This way he'll grow virtuously into wisdom.

What are we waiting for, packed in the forum?

    The barbarians are due here today.

Why isn't anything going on in the senate?
Why have the senators given up legislating?

    Because the barbarians are coming today.
    What's the point of senators and their laws now?
    When the barbarians get here, they'll do the
        legislating.

Why did our emperor set out so early
to sit on his throne at the city's main gate,
in state, wearing the crown?

    Because the barbarians are coming today
    and the emperor's waiting to receive their leader.
    He's even got a citation to give him,
    loaded with titles and imposing names.

Why have our two consuls and praetors shown up today
wearing their embroidered, their scarlet togas?
Why have they put on bracelets with so many amethysts,
rings sparkling with all those emeralds?
Why are they carrying elegant canes
so beautifully worked in silver and gold?

      Because the barbarians are coming today
      and things like that dazzle barbarians.

And why don't our distinguished orators push forward as
      usual
to make their speeches, say what they have to say?

      Because the barbarians are coming today
      and they're bored by rhetoric and public speaking.

Why this sudden bewilderment, this confusion?
(How serious everyone looks.)
Why are the streets and squares rapidly emptying,
everyone going home so lost in thought?

      Because it's night and the barbarians haven't come.
      And some people just in from the border say
      there are no barbarians any longer.

Now what's going to happen to us without them?
The barbarians were a kind of solution.

Our efforts are those of men prone to disaster;
our efforts are like those of the Trojans.
We just begin to get somewhere,
begin to gather a little strength,
grow almost bold and hopeful,

when something always comes up to stop us:
Achilles leaps out of the trench in front of us
and terrifies us with his violent shouting.

Our efforts are like those of the Trojans.
We think we'll change our luck
by being resolute and brave,
so we move outside ready to fight.

But when the great crisis comes,
our boldness and resolution vanish;
our spirit falters, collapses,
and we scurry around the walls
trying to save ourselves by running away.

Yet we're sure to fail. Up there,
high on the walls, the dirge has already begun.
They're mourning the memory, the aura of our days.
Priam and Hecuba mourn for us bitterly.

Not like a king but an actor he put on a gray cloak instead
of his royal one and secretly went away.

PLUTARCH, *Life of Dimitrios*

When the Macedonians deserted him
and showed they preferred Pyrrhos,
noble King Dimitrios didn't behave
—so it was said—
at all like a king.
He took off his golden robes,
discarded his purple buskins,
and quickly dressing himself
in simple clothes, he slipped out—
just like an actor who,
the play over,
changes his costume and goes away.

But when he heard the women wailing,
lamenting his sorry state—
madam with her oriental gestures
and her slaves with their barbarous Greek—
the pride in his soul rose up,
his Italian blood sickened with disgust
and all he'd worshipped blindly till then—
his wild Alexandrian life—
now seemed dull and alien.
And he said: "Stop wailing for me.
It's all wrong, that kind of thing.
You ought to be singing my praises
for having been a great ruler,
a man of wealth and glory.
And if I'm down now, I haven't fallen humbly,
but as a Roman conquered by a Roman."

Eagles of coral
adorn the ebony bed
where Nero lies deep in sleep—
callous, peaceful, and happy,
robust in the vigor of his flesh
and the full vitality of youth.

But in the alabaster hall that keeps
the ancient shrine of the Aenobarbi
how restless the household gods!
The little creatures tremble
and try to hide their insignificant bodies.
They've heard a frightening sound,
a deadly sound coming up the stairs,
iron footsteps that shake the staircase;
and faint with fear, the miserable Lares
scramble to the back of the shrine,
shoving each other and stumbling,
one little god falling over another,
because they know what kind of sound that is,
they recognize by now the footsteps of the Furies.

You said: "I'll go to some other place, some other sea,
find another city better than this one.
Every move I make is doomed to come out wrong
and my heart, like something dead, lies buried inside me.
How long is my mind to wither away like this?
Wherever I turn, wherever I look,
I see the black ruin of my life, here,
where I've spent so many years—wasted, destroyed them
    utterly."

You won't find some other place, some other sea.
The city will follow you. And you'll walk
the same streets, grow old in the same neighborhood,
in these same houses watch yourself turn gray.
You'll always end up in this city. Don't look for things
    elsewhere:
there's no ship for you, no road out.
Just as you've ruined your life here, in this small corner,
you've destroyed it now everywhere in the world.

THE SATRAPY*

Too bad that, cut out as you are
for fine and noble things,
this unfair fate of yours
never gives you a chance, never provides what you want;
that vulgar habits get in your way,
pettiness and indifference.
And how terrible the day you give in
(the day you let go and give in)
and take the road for Susa
to find King Artaxerxes,
who graciously places you in his court
and offers you satrapies and things like that—
things you don't want at all,
though, despairingly, you accept them all the same.
Your heart longs for something else, aches for other things:
praise from the crowd and the Sophists,
that hard-won, that priceless acclaim—
the Agora, the theatre, the crowns of laurel.
You can't get these from Artaxerxes,
you'll never find these in the satrapy,
and without them, what kind of life will you live?

My soul, guard against pomp and glory.
And if you can't curb your ambitions,
at least pursue them hesitantly, cautiously.
And the higher you go,
the more searching and careful you need to be.

And when you reach your summit, Caesar at last—
when you assume the role of someone as great as that—
be really careful as you go out into the street,
a conspicuous man of power with your retinue;
and should a certain Artemidoros
come up to you out of the crowd, bringing a letter,
and say hurriedly: "Read this right away.
It's about you, and it's vitally important,"
be sure to stop; be sure to put off
all talk or business; be sure to keep clear
of those who salute and bow to you
(they can be seen later); let even
the Senate itself wait—and find out at once
what vital news Artemidoros has written down for you.

Tortured by fear and suspicion,
mind agitated, eyes alarmed,
we invent ways out,
plan how to avoid
the inevitable danger that threatens us so terribly.
And yet we're mistaken, there's a different danger ahead:
the news was wrong
(or we didn't hear it, or didn't get it right).
Another disaster, one we never imagined,
suddenly, violently, overwhelms us,
and finding us unprepared—there's no time now—
sweeps us away.

At midnight, when suddenly you hear
an invisible procession going past
with exquisite music, voices,
don't mourn your luck that's failing now,
work gone wrong, your plans
all proving deceptive—don't mourn them uselessly:
as though long prepared, and full of courage,
say goodbye to her, to Alexandria who is leaving.
Above all, don't fool yourself, don't say
it was a dream, that your ears deceived you:
don't degrade yourself with empty hopes like these.
As though long prepared, and full of courage,
as though natural in you who've been given this kind of city,
go firmly to the window
and listen with emotion,
but not with the regret, the whinings of a coward,
listen—your final pleasure—to the voices,
to the exquisite music of that strange procession,
and say goodbye to her, to the Alexandria you are losing.

IONIC

That we've broken their statues,
that we've driven them out of their temples
doesn't mean at all that the gods are dead.
O land of Ionia, they're still in love with you,
their souls still keep your memory.
When an August dawn wakes over you,
the atmosphere is potent with their life
and sometimes a young ethereal figure
indistinct, in rapid flight,
wings across your hills.

When you set out for Ithaka
pray that your road's a long one,
full of adventure, full of discovery.
Laistrygonians, Cyclops,
angry Poseidon—don't be scared of them:
you won't find things like that on your way
as long as your thoughts are exalted,
as long as a rare excitement
stirs your spirit and your body.
Laistrygonians, Cyclops,
wild Poseidon—you won't encounter them
unless you bring them along inside you,
unless your soul raises them up in front of you.

Pray that your road's a long one.
May there be many a summer morning when—
full of gratitude, full of joy—
you come into harbors seen for the first time;
may you stop at Phoenician trading centers
and buy fine things,
mother of pearl and coral, amber and ebony,
sensual perfumes of every kind,
as many sensual perfumes as you can;
may you visit numerous Egyptian cities
to fill yourself with learning from the wise.

Keep Ithaka always in mind.
Arriving there is what you're destined for.
But don't hurry the journey at all.
Better if it goes on for years
so you're old by the time you reach the island,
wealthy with all you've gained on the way,
not expecting Ithaka to make you rich.

Ithaka gave you the marvelous journey.
Without her you wouldn't have set out.
She hasn't anything else to give.

And if you find her poor, Ithaka won't have fooled you.
Wise as you'll have become, and so experienced,
you'll have understood by then what an Ithaka means.

Make sure the engraving is done skillfully.
The expression serious and majestic.
The crown preferably somewhat narrow:
I don't like the broad Parthian type.
The inscription, as usual, in Greek:
Nothing excessive or pompous—
we don't want the proconsul to take it the wrong way;
he's always smelling things out and reporting back to
    Rome—
but of course properly respectful.
Something very special on the other side:
a discus-thrower, young, good-looking.
Above all I urge you to see to it
(Sithaspis, for God's sake, don't let them forget)
that after "King" and "Savior",
they add "Philhellene" in elegant characters.
Now don't try to be clever
with your "where are the Greeks?" and "what Hellenism
here behind Zagros, out beyond Phraata?"
Since so many others more barbarian than ourselves
choose to inscribe it, we'll inscribe it too.
And besides, don't forget that sometimes
sophists do come to us from Syria,
and versifiers, and other triflers.
So we're not, I think, un-Hellenized.

The Alexandrians had gathered
to see Cleopatra's children,
Kaisarion and his younger brothers,
Alexander and Ptolemy,
who'd been taken out to the Gymnasium for the first time,
to be proclaimed kings there
before a brilliant array of soldiers.

Alexander: they declared him
king of Armenia, Midia, and the Parthians.
Ptolemy: they declared him
king of Cilicia, Syria, and Phoenicia.
Kaisarion was standing in front of the others,
dressed in pink silk,
on his chest a bunch of hyacinths,
his belt a double row of sapphires and amethysts,
his shoes tied with white ribbons
prinked with rose-colored pearls.
They declared him greater than his brothers,
they declared him King of Kings.

The Alexandrians knew of course
that this was just talk and show-business.

But the day was warm and poetic,
the sky a pale blue,
the Alexandrian Gymnasium
a triumphant artistic success,
the courtiers wonderfully sumptuous,
Kaisarion all grace and beauty
(Cleopatra's son, blood of the Lagids);
and the Alexandrians thronged to the festival,
and were enthusiastic, and shouted acclamations
in Greek, and Egyptian, and some in Hebrew,
charmed by the lovely spectacle—
though of course they knew what all this was worth,
what empty words they really were, these kingships.

An old man—used up, bent,
crippled by time and abuse—
slowly walks along the narrow street.
But as he goes inside his house to hide
the shambles of his old age, his thoughts fix
on the share in youth that still belongs to him.

His verse is now quoted by young men.
His images come before their lively eyes.
Their healthy sensual minds,
their shapely well-knit bodies
stir to his vision of the beautiful.

Even if you can't shape your life the way you want,
at least try as much as you can
not to cheapen it totally
by too much contact with the world
and all its traffic and talk.

Don't degrade it by dragging it along,
taking it around and exposing it so often
to the daily silliness
of meetings and parties
until it comes to seem unbearable,
no longer your own.

RETURNING FROM GREECE

Well, we're nearly there, Hermippos.
Day after tomorrow, it seems—that's what the captain said.
At least we're sailing our seas,
the waters of Cyprus, of Syria and Egypt,
cherished waters of our own countries.
Why so quiet? Ask your heart:
didn't you too feel happier
the further we got from Greece?
What's the point of fooling ourselves?
That, of course, wouldn't be properly Hellenic.

It's time we admitted the truth:
we're Greeks also—what else are we?—
but with Asiatic tastes and feelings,
tastes and feelings
sometimes repugnant to Hellenism.

It isn't right, Hermippos, for us philosophers
to be like some of our petty kings
(remember how we laughed at them
when they used to come to our lectures?)
who through their showy Hellenified exteriors
(Macedonian exteriors, naturally)
let a bit of Arabia peep out now and then,
a bit of Midia they can't keep back.
And what comic artifice the fools used
trying to cover it up!

No, that's not at all right for us.
For Greeks like us that kind of pettiness won't do.
We mustn't be ashamed
of the Syrian and Egyptian blood in our veins:
we should honor it, we should glory in it.

It goes on being Alexandria still. Just walk a bit
along its straight road ending at the Hippodrome
and you'll see palaces and monuments that will amaze you.
Whatever war-damage it's suffered,
however much smaller it's grown,
it's still a wonderful city.
And then, what with excursions and books
and various kinds of study, time does go by.
In the evenings we meet on the seafront,
the five of us (all, naturally, under fictitious names)
and some of the few other Greeks
still left in the city.
Sometimes we discuss church affairs
(the people here seem to lean toward Rome)
and sometimes literature.
The other day we read some lines by Nonnos:
what imagery, what rhythm, what diction and harmony!
In our enthusiasm, how we admired the Panopolitan.
So the days go by, and our stay here
isn't unpleasant because, naturally,
it's not going to last forever.
We've had good news: whether
something is happening now in Smyrna, or whether
in April our friends decide to move from Epiros,
our plans are definitely working out, and we'll easily
    overthrow Basil.
And when we do, at last our turn will come.

If you're really one of the chosen few,
watch how you attain your eminence.
No matter how much you're acclaimed, how much
the cities praise your achievements
in Italy and Thessaly,
whatever honors
your admirers decree for you in Rome,
your joy, your triumph won't last,
nor will you feel superior—hardly superior!—
when in Alexandria Theodotos brings you,
on a blood-stained tray,
miserable Pompey's head.

And don't be too sure that in your life—
restricted, regulated, prosaic—
spectacular and horrible things like that don't happen.
Maybe this very moment Theodotos—
bodiless, invisible—
is carrying into some neighbor's tidy house
an equally repulsive head.

He swears every now and then to begin a better life.
But when night comes with its own promptings,
its own compromises and prospects—
when night comes with its own power
of bodily desires and longings,
he returns, lost, to the same fatal pleasure.

I'll stop here, and I'll look at nature awhile.
The brilliant blue of the morning sea, of the cloudless sky,
the shore yellow: all lovely,
all bathed in light.

I'll stand here. And I'll make myself believe that I really see
    all this
(I actually did see it for a minute when I first stopped)
and not my usual day-dreams here too,
memories, my images of sensuality.

The figure on this four drachma coin
who seems to have a smile on his face—
his beautiful, delicate face—
this figure is Orophernis, son of Ariarathis.

A child, they threw him out of Cappadocia,
out of his great ancestral palace,
and sent him to grow up in Ionia,
to be forgotten there among foreigners.

Oh those superb Ionian nights
when fearlessly, and entirely in a Greek way,
he learned all there is to know about making love.
In his heart, Asiatic always,
but in manners and language, a Greek;
with his turquoise jewelry, his Greek clothes,
his body perfumed with jasmine scent,
he was the most handsome, the most perfect
of Ionia's exquisite young men.

Later, when the Syrians entered Cappadocia
and made him king,
he became fully engrossed in his kingship
in order to find some new pleasure each day,
greedily hoarding gold and silver,
delightedly gloating over
the piles of wealth glittering before his eyes.

As for worrying about the country and running it—
he didn't have a clue what was going on.
The Cappadocians quickly got rid of him,
and he ended up in Syria, at the palace of Dimitrios,
where he spent his time amusing himself and loafing.

But one day unfamiliar thoughts
broke in on his complete idleness:
he remembered how through his mother Antiochis
and that old grandmother Stratoniki
he too was connected with the Syrian crown,
he too almost a Selefkid.
For a while he gave up lechery and drink
and ineptly, half dazed,
tried to start an intrigue,
do something, come up with a plan;
but he failed pitifully and that was that.

His end must have been recorded somewhere only to be
    lost;
or maybe history passed over it
and rightly didn't bother to notice
something so trivial.

The figure who has left on this four drachma coin
some of the charm of his lovely youth,
a ray of his poetic beauty,
a sensuous glimpse of an Ionian boy,
this figure is Orophernis, son of Ariarathis.

He's lost his old fire, his courage.
Now his tired body, almost sick,

will be his first concern. And he'll spend
what life he has left without worrying. So Philip says,
  anyway.

Tonight he's playing a game with dice;
he's in a mood to enjoy himself.

Cover the table with roses. What if Antiochos
was annihilated at Magnesia? They say

the bulk of his brilliant army was totally crushed.
Maybe they're stretching it a bit; it can't all be true.

Let's hope so. Because though enemies, we do belong to
  the same race.
But one "let's hope so" is enough. Maybe even too much.

Philip of course won't put off the festivities.
However much his life has worn him out,

one blessing remains: his memory hasn't weakened at all.
He remembers how much they mourned in Syria, the kind
  of sorrow they felt,

when Macedonia, their motherland, was smashed to pieces.
Let the banquet begin. Slaves! The music, the lights!

One sad September day
Emperor Manuel Komninos
felt that his death was near.
The court astrologers—paid, of course—insisted
that he still had many years to live.
But while they were having their say,
he remembered a pious ancient custom
and ordered ecclesiastical vestments
to be brought from a monastery,
and he put them on, glad to appear
modestly dressed like a priest or monk.

Happy those who believe,
and like Emperor Manuel end their lives
dressed so modestly in the vestments of their faith.

Dimitrios Selefkidis was upset
to learn that a Ptolemy
had reached Italy in such a shameful state:
poorly dressed and on foot,
only three or four slaves. This way
their house will become a joke,
the laughter of Rome.
Selefkidis of course knows
that basically even now they're something like servants
to the Romans; he also knows
that the Romans give and take away
their thrones arbitrarily, as they please.
But they should maintain a certain dignity
at least in their appearance;
they shouldn't forget that they're still kings,
still (alas) called kings.

This is why Dimitrios Selefkidis was upset;
and right away he offered Ptolemy
purple robes, a magnificent diadem,
precious jewels, numerous servants and retainers,
his finest horses,
so that he might present himself at Rome as he should,
as an Alexandrian Greek monarch.

But Ptolemy, who'd come to beg for aid,
knew what he was up to and refused it all:
he didn't have the slightest need for these luxuries.
Shabbily dressed, humble, he entered Rome,
scrounged a bed in the house of a minor artisan,
and then he presented himself
as a sorry pauper to the Senate
in order to make his begging more effective.

Raphael, they're asking you to write a few lines
as an epitaph for the poet Ammonis:
something very tasteful and polished. You can do it,
you're the one to write something suitable
for the poet Ammonis, our Ammonis.

Of course you'll speak about his poems—
but say something too about his beauty,
about that subtle beauty we loved so much.

Your Greek is always elegant and musical.
But we want all your craftsmanship now.
Our sorrow and our love move into a foreign language.
Empty your Egyptian feeling into the Greek you use.

Raphael, your verses, you know, should be written
so they contain something of our life within them,
so the rhythm, so every phrase clearly shows
that an Alexandrian is writing about an Alexandrian.

When one of them moved through the center of Selefkia
just as it was getting dark—
moved like a young man, tall, extremely handsome,
the joy of immortality in his eyes,
his hair black and perfumed—
the people going by would gaze at him,
and they would ask each other who he was,
if he was a Greek from Syria, or a stranger.
But some who looked more carefully
would understand and step aside;
and as he disappeared under the colonnade,
among the shadows and the evening lights,
going toward the quarter that lives
only at night, with orgies and debauchery,
with every kind of intoxication and desire,
they would wonder which of Them it could be,
and for what suspicious pleasure
he'd come down into the streets of Selefkia
from the August Celestial Mansions.

I never had you nor, I suppose,
will I ever have you. A few words, an approach,
as in the bar yesterday—nothing more.
It's sad, I admit. But we who serve Art,
sometimes with the mind's intensity
can create pleasure that's almost physical—
but of course only for a short time.
That's how in the bar yesterday—
mercifully helped by alcohol—
I had half an hour that was totally erotic.
And I think you understood this
and stayed slightly longer on purpose.
It was very necessary, that. Because
with all the imagination, all the magic alcohol,
I needed to see your lips as well,
needed your body near me.

Partly to refresh my memory of a historical period,
partly to kill an hour or two,
last night I picked up and read
a volume of inscriptions about the Ptolemies.
The lavish praise and flattery are much the same
for each of them. All are brilliant,
glorious, mighty, benevolent;
everything they undertake is full of wisdom.
As for the women of their line, the Berenices and
    Cleopatras,
they too, all of them, are marvelous.

When I'd found what I wanted
I would have put the book away, but a brief
insignificant mention of King Kaisarion
suddenly caught my eye . . .

There you stood with your indefinable charm.
Because we know
so little about you from history,
I could picture you more freely in my mind.
I pictured you good-looking and sensitive.
My art gives your face
a dreamy, appealing beauty.
And so completely did I imagine you
that late last night,
as my lamp went out—I let it go out on purpose—
I thought you came into my room,
it seemed you stood there in front of me, stood as you would
    have
in conquered Alexandria,
pale and weary, ideal in your grief,
still hoping they might take pity on you,
those bastards who whispered: "Too many Caesars."

Body, remember not only how much you were loved,
not only the beds on which you lay,
but also those desires glowing openly
in eyes that looked at you,
trembling for you in voices that spoke to you—
only some chance obstacle frustrated them.
Now that it's all finally in the past,
it seems almost as if you gave yourself
to those desires too—how they glowed,
remember, in eyes that looked at you,
remember, body, how they trembled for you in those voices.

NERO'S RESPITE*

Nero wasn't worried when he heard
the pronouncement of the Delphic Oracle:
"Beware the age of seventy-three."
Plenty of time to enjoy himself.
He's thirty. The respite
the god has given him is quite enough
to cope with future dangers.

Now, a little tired, he'll return to Rome—
but wonderfully tired after that journey
devoted entirely to pleasure:
theaters, garden-parties, stadiums. . .
evenings in the cities of Achaia. . .
above all the delight of naked bodies. . .

So Nero muses. And in Spain Galba
secretly musters and drills his army—
Galba, now in his seventy-third year.

For centuries they hadn't seen gifts at Delphi
as fine as those sent by the two brothers,
the rival Ptolemaic kings. But now that they have them,
the priests get nervous about the oracle.
They'll need all their experience
to determine subtly which of the two—
which of two brothers like these—will have to be offended.
And so they meet secretly at night
to discuss the personal affairs of the Lagids.

But suddenly the envoys are back. They're taking their
    leave.
Returning to Alexandria, they say. And they don't ask
for an oracle at all. The priests are delighted to hear it
(they're to keep the marvelous gifts, that goes without
    saying)
but they're also totally bewildered,
not having a clue what this sudden indifference means.
They don't know that yesterday the envoys received serious
    news:
the "oracle" was pronounced in Rome; it was there the
    dispute was settled.

AIMILIANOS MONAI, ALEXANDRIAN, A.D. 628-655

Out of talk, appearance, and manners
I'll make an excellent suit of armor;
and in this way I'll face malicious people
without fear or weakness.

They'll try to injure me. But of those
who come near me none will know
where to find my wounds, my vulnerable places,
under the deceptions that will cover me.

So boasted Aimilianos Monai.
One wonders if he ever made that suit of armor.
Anyway, he didn't wear it long.
At the age of twenty-seven, he died in Sicily.

I know this room so well.
Now they're renting it, and the one next to it,
as offices. The whole house has become
an office building for agents, and tradesmen, and companies.

This room, how familiar it is.

The couch was here, near the door,
a Turkish carpet in front of it.
Close by, the shelf with two yellow vases.
On the right—no, opposite—a wardrobe with a mirror.
In the middle the table where he wrote,
and the three big wicker chairs.
Beside the window the bed
where we made love so many times.

They must still be around somewhere, those old things.

Beside the window the bed;
The afternoon sun used to touch half of it.

. . . Four o'clock in the afternoon we separated
for a week only . . . And then—
the week became forever.

Painter and poet, runner, discus-thrower,
beautiful as Endymion: Ianthis, son of Antony.
From a family on close terms with the Synagogue.

"My noblest days are those
when I give up the search for sensation,
when I desert brilliant and harsh Hellenism,
with its commanding devotion
to perfectly shaped, corruptible white limbs,
and become the man I would want to remain forever:
son of the Jews, the holy Jews."

A most fervent declaration on his part: ". . . to remain
   forever
a son of the Jews, the holy Jews."

But he didn't remain anything of the kind.
The Hedonism and Art of Alexandria
possessed him as their dedicated son.

Everything he'd hoped for had gone wrong.

He'd seen himself doing great things,
ending the humiliation that had kept his country down
ever since the battle of Magnesia—
seen himself making Syria a powerful state once more,
with her armies, her fleets,
her big fortresses, her wealth.

He'd suffered in Rome, become bitter
when he sensed in the talk of his friends,
young men of the great families,
that in spite of all their delicacy and politeness
toward him, the son
of King Selefkos Philopatir—
when he sensed that in spite of this there was always
a secret contempt for the Hellenizing dynasties:
their time was over, they weren't fit for anything serious,
were completely unable to rule anyone.
He'd struggled on alone, become angry, and had sworn
it would be quite different from the way they thought.
Why, wasn't he himself full of determination?
He would act, he would fight, he would set it all right again.

If he could only find a way of getting to the East,
only manage to escape from Italy,
then all this inner strength,
all this energy,
he'd pass on to the people.

Only to be in Syria!
He was so young when he left his country
he hardly remembered what it looked like.
But in his mind he'd always seen it
as something sacred that you approach reverently,
as a beautiful place unveiled, a vision
of Greek cities and Greek ports.

And now?
        Now despair and sorrow.

They were right, the young men in Rome.
The dynasties resulting from the Macedonian Conquest
can't go on any longer.

It doesn't matter. He'd made the effort,
fought as much as he could.
And in his black disillusion
there's still one thing he's proud of:
that even in his failure
he shows the world his same indomitable courage.

For the rest, they were dreams and wasted energy.
This Syria almost doesn't seem to be his country—
this Syria is the land of Valas and Herakleidis.

"Where did the Sage retreat to, where did he disappear?
After his many miracles,
the renown of his teaching
which spread to so many countries,
he suddenly hid himself and nobody knew
for certain what became of him
(nor did anybody ever see his grave).
Some claimed he died at Ephesus.
But Damis doesn't say so in his memoir.
Damis says nothing about the death of Apollonius.
Others reported that he disappeared at Lindos.
Or maybe the story is true
about his assumption in Crete,
at the ancient sanctuary of Diktynna.
And then again we have that miraculous,
that supernatural apparition of his
before a young student at Tyana.
Maybe the time hasn't yet come for him to return
and show himself to the world again;
or maybe, transfigured, he moves among us
unrecognized——. But he will come again
as he was, teaching the truth; and then of course
he will bring back the worship of our gods
and our elegant Hellenic rites."

So mused in his shabby room one of the few pagans,
one of the very few who still remained,
having just read
Philostratos' *On Apollonios of Tyana*.
But even he—a trivial and cowardly man—
played the Christian in public and went to church.
It was the time when Justin the Elder
reigned in total piety,
and Alexandria, a godly city,
detested pitiful idolators.

The actor they'd brought in to entertain them
also recited a few choice epigrams.

The room opened out on an upper garden
and a delicate smell of flowers
mingled with the scent
of the five perfumed young Sidonians.

There were readings from Meleager, Krinagoras, Rhianos.
But when the actor recited
"Here lies Aeschylus, son of Euphorion, an Athenian"
(stressing maybe more than he should have
"his renowned valor" and "Marathonian grove"),
a vivacious young man, mad about literature,
suddenly cut in and said:

"I don't like that quatrain at all.
Sentiments of that kind seem somehow weak.
You should give, I say, all your strength to your work,
make it your total concern. And you should still remember
    your work
in time of stress or when you begin to decline.
This is what I expect, what I demand of you—
and not that you completely dismiss
your magnificent tragedies—
your *Agamemnon*, your marvelous *Prometheus*,
your representations of Orestes and Cassandra,
your *Seven Against Thebes*—merely to set down for your
    memorial
that as an ordinary soldier, one of the herd,
you too fought against Datis and Artaphernis."

Phernazis the poet is at work
on the important part of his epic:
how Dareios, son of Hystaspis,
took over the Persian kingdom.
(It's from him, Dareios, that our glorious king,
Mithridatis, Dionysos, and Evpator, descends.)
But this calls for serious thought; he has to analyze
the feelings Dareios must have had:
arrogance, maybe, and intoxication? No—more likely
a certain insight into the vanities of greatness.
The poet ponders the matter deeply.

But his servant, running in,
cuts him short to announce very important news.
The war with the Romans has begun.
Most of our army has crossed the borders.

The poet is dumbfounded. What a disaster!
How can our glorious king,
Mithridatis, Dionysos, and Evpator,
bother about Greek poems now?
In the middle of a war—just think, Greek poems!

Phernazis gets worked up. What a bad break!
Just when he was sure to distinguish himself
with his *Dareios*, sure to make
his envious critics shut up once and for all.
What a postponement, terrible postponement of his plans.

And if it's only a postponement, that would be fine.
But are we really safe in Amisos?
The town isn't very well fortified,
and the Romans are the most awful enemies.
Are we, Cappadocians, really a match for them?
Is it conceivable?
Are we to compete with the legions?
Great gods, protectors of Asia, help us.

But through all his distress and agitation
the poetic idea comes and goes insistently:
arrogance and intoxication—that's the most likely, of
    course:
arrogance and intoxication are what Dareios must have felt.

ANNA KOMNINA*

In the prologue to her *Alexiad*,
Anna Komnina laments her widowhood.

Her soul is all in vertigo.
"And I bathe my eyes," she tells us,
"in rivers of tears. . . . Alas for the waves" of her life,
"alas for the revolutions." Sorrow burns her
"to the bones and the marrow and the dividing of her soul."

But the truth seems to be this power-hungry woman
knew only one sorrow that really mattered;
even if she doesn't admit it, this arrogant Greek woman
was deeply upset about one thing only:
that with all her cunning,
she never managed to gain the throne,
virtually snatched out of her hands by impudent John.

AN EXILED BYZANTINE NOBLEMAN
WHO COMPOSES VERSES*

————————————————————————

The frivolous can call me frivolous.
I've always taken important things
extremely seriously. And I insist that no one knows
the Holy Fathers, or the Scriptures, or the Conciliar Canons
better than I do.
In each of his doubts,
in every ecclesiastical difficulty,
Botaniatis consulted me, me first of all.
But exiled here (she'd better watch out, that hellcat
Irini Doukaina), and incredibly bored,
it's not altogether unfitting to amuse myself
writing six- and eight-line verses,
to amuse myself with the mythology
of Hermes and Apollo and Dionysos,
or the heroes of Thessaly and the Peloponnese;
and to compose correct iambics,
such as—if you'll allow me to say so—
the scholars of Constantinople don't know how to compose.
It may be just this correctness that makes them condemn me.

I'm not the slightest bit put out that my chariot wheel broke
and I lost that silly race.
I'll drink great wines the whole night,
lying among roses. Antioch is all mine.
I'm the most celebrated young man in town—
Valas' weakness, he simply adores me.
You'll see, tomorrow they'll say the race wasn't fair
(though if I'd been vulgar enough to insist on it secretly,
the flatterers would have given first place even to my
    limping chariot).

His subject, "The Character of Dimaratos",
which Porphyry proposed to him in conversation
and which he planned to develop rhetorically later,
was outlined by the young sophist as follows:

"First a courtier of King Dareios,
and after that of King Xerxes,
now with Xerxes and his army,
at last Dimaratos will have his revenge.

Great the injustice done him.
He was Ariston's son. His enemies
bribed the oracle brazenly.
And it wasn't enough that they denied him his kingship,
but when he finally gave in and decided
to live patiently as a private citizen,
they had to insult him even before the people,
they had to humiliate him publicly at the festival.

As a result, he serves Xerxes assiduously.
Along with the great Persian army,
he'll get back to Sparta too;
and once he's king again, how quickly
he'll throw him out, how thoroughly
he'll break that schemer Leotychidis.

So now he's on the go from morning till night
advising the Persians, explaining
what they should do to conquer Greece.

Much worry, much thinking, and for this reason
Dimaratos finds his days such a burden;
much worry, much thinking, and for this reason
Dimaratos can't find a moment's joy—
because what he's feeling can't be called joy
(it isn't; he won't admit it;
how can he call it joy? his position couldn't be worse)
now that things clearly show him
it's the Greeks who are going to win."

For two years he studied with Ammonios Sakkas,
but was bored by both philosophy and Sakkas.

Then he went into politics.
But he gave that up. The Prefect was a fool,
and those around him solemn, officious nitwits:
their Greek—the idiots—was hopeless.

After that he became
vaguely curious about the Church: to be baptized
and pass as a Christian. But he soon
let that one drop: it would certainly have caused a row
with his parents, showy pagans,
and right away they would have stopped—a terrible
    thing—
their extremely generous allowance.

But he had to do something. He began to haunt
the corrupt houses of Alexandria,
every secret den of debauchery.

Here he was lucky:
he'd been given an extremely handsome figure.
And he enjoyed the divine gift.

His looks would last
at least another ten years. And after that?
Maybe he'll go back to Sakkas.
Or if the old man has died meanwhile,
he'll find another philosopher or sophist:
there's always someone suitable around.

Or in the end he might possibly return
even to politics—commendably remembering
the traditions of his family,
duty toward the country, and all that junk.

"Observing, then, that there is great contempt for the gods
among us"—he says in his solemn way.
Contempt. But what did he expect?
Let him organize religion as much as he liked,
write to the High Priest of Galatia as much as he liked,
or to others of his kind, inciting and guiding them.
His friends weren't Christians; that much was definite.
But even so they couldn't play
as he could (brought up a Christian)
with a new religious system,
ludicrous in theory and application.
They were, after all, Greeks. Nothing in excess, Augustus.

EPITAPH OF ANTIOCHOS,
KING OF KOMMAGINI*

58 ──

After the funeral of the scholarly Antiochos, King of
    Kommagini,
whose life had been restrained and gentle,
his sister, deeply afflicted,
wanted an epitaph for him;
and on the suggestion of the Syrian courtiers,
the Ephesian sophist Kallistratos (who often resided
in the small state of Kommagini
and was a welcome and frequent guest
at the royal house)
wrote it and sent it to the old lady.

"People of Kommagini, let the glory of Antiochos,
the noble king, be celebrated as it deserves.
He was a provident ruler of the country.
He was just, wise, courageous.
In addition he was that superlative thing, Hellenic—
mankind has no finer quality:
everything beyond that belongs to the gods."

From his village near the outskirts of town,
still dust-covered from the journey in,

the peddler arrives. And "Incense!" "Gum!"
"The best olive oil!" "Perfume for your hair!"

he hawks through the streets. But with all the hubbub,
the music, the parades, who can hear him?

The crowd shoves him around, drags him along, crushes
  him.
And when he asks, now totally confused, "What the hell's
  going on here?"

one of them tosses him the huge palace lie:
that Antony is winning in Greece.

He sees the fields that still belong to him:
the wheat, the animals, the trees laden with fruit;
and beyond them his ancestral home
full of clothes, and costly furniture, and silverware.

They'll take them away from him—O God—they'll take
   them away from him now.

Would Kantakuzinos show pity for him
if he went and fell at his feet? They say he's merciful,
very merciful. But those around him? And the army?—
Or should he fall down and plead before Lady Irini?

Fool that he was to get mixed up in Anna's party!
If only Lord Andronikos had never married her!
Has anything good come from the way she's behaved,
   any humanity?
Even the Franks don't respect her any longer.
Her plans were ridiculous, her preparations farcical.
While they were threatening everyone from Constantinople,
Kantakuzinos demolished them, Lord John demolished
   them.

And to think he'd planned to join
Lord John's party! And he would have done it, and would
   have been happy now,
a great nobleman still, his position secure,
if the bishop hadn't dissuaded him at the last moment
with his imposing hieratic manner,
his completely bogus information,
his promises and all his phony talk.

I'm very moved by one detail
in the coronation at Vlachernai of John Kantakuzinos
and Irini, daughter of Andronikos Asan.
Because they were short of precious stones
(our troubled empire was extremely poor)
they wore artificial ones: clusters of glass fragments,
red, green, and blue. I find
nothing humiliating or undignified
in those little pieces of colored glass.
Just the opposite: they seem
a sad protest against
the unjust poverty of the crowned couple,
symbols of what they deserved to have,
of what surely it was right that they have
at their coronation—a Lord John Kantakuzinos,
a Lady Irini, daughter of Andronikos Asan.

He goes regularly to the taverna
where they'd met the previous month.
He made inquiries, but they weren't able to tell him
    anything.
From what they said, he gathered the person he'd met
was someone totally unknown,
one of the many unknown and suspect young figures
that dropped in there.
But he still goes to the taverna regularly, at night,
and sits there gazing toward the doorway,
gazing toward the doorway until he's worn out.
Maybe he'll walk in. Tonight maybe he'll show up.

He does this for nearly three weeks.
His mind is sick from longing.
The kisses have stayed on his mouth.
All of his flesh suffers from unremitting desire.
The touch of that body is on him,
he wants to be joined with it again.

Of course he tries not to give himself away.
But sometimes it hardly seems to matter.
Besides, he knows what he's exposing himself to,
he's come to accept it: very possibly this life of his
will lead to some scandalous disaster.

Kleitos, a likeable young man,
about twenty-three years old—
with a first-class education, an unusual knowledge of
    Greek—
is seriously ill. He caught the fever
that reaped a harvest this year in Alexandria.

The fever found him morally worn out
by the pain of knowing that his friend, a young actor,
had stopped loving and wanting him.

He's seriously ill, and his parents tremble with fear.

An old servant who brought him up
also trembles with fear for Kleitos' life;
and in her terrible panic
she remembers an idol she used to worship
when she was young, before she came there as a maid,
to the house of distinguished Christians, and turned
    Christian herself.
She secretly brings some votive bread, some wine and
    honey
and places them before the idol. She chants whatever
    phrases
she remembers from prayers: odds and ends. The ninny
doesn't realize that the black demon couldn't care less
whether a Christian gets well or not.

The news from Actium, about the outcome of the sea-battle,
was of course unexpected.
But there's no need for us to draw up a new proclamation.
The name's the only thing that has to be changed.
There, in the concluding lines, instead of: "Having freed
   the Romans
from Octavius, that disaster,
that parody of a Caesar,"
we'll substitute: "Having freed the Romans
from Antony, that disaster, . . ."
The whole text fits very nicely.

"To the most glorious victor,
matchless in the field of battle,
prodigious in his political operations,
on whose behalf the township ardently wished
for Antony's triumph, . . ."
here, as we said, the substitution: "for Octavius' triumph,
regarding it Zeus' greatest gift—
to this mighty protector of the Greeks,
who graciously honors Greek customs,
who is beloved in every Greek domain,
who is clearly destined for exalted praise,
and whose exploits should be recorded at length
in the Greek language, in both verse and prose,
in the *Greek language*, the vehicle of fame,"
et cetera, et cetera. It all fits brilliantly.

A GREAT PROCESSION OF
PRIESTS AND LAYMEN *

A procession of priests and laymen—
each walk of life represented—
moves through streets and squares and gates
of the famous city of Antioch.
At the head of this imposing procession
a handsome white-clad boy
carries the Cross, his arms held high—
our strength and hope, the holy Cross.
The pagans, lately so full of arrogance,
have lost their nerve and, cowards now,
slink away from the procession.
Let them keep their distance, always keep their distance
    from us
(as long as they don't renounce their delusions).
The holy Cross goes forward, bringing joy and consolation
to every quarter where God-fearing Christians live;
and elated now they stand in their doorways to greet it:
the strength, the salvation of the universe, the Cross.

This is an annual Christian festival.
But today, you see, it's more spectacular.
The empire is delivered at last.
The thoroughly depraved, the appalling Julian
reigns no longer.

For most pious Jovian let us give our prayers.

Neither the letter C, they say, nor the letter K had ever
harmed the city . . . We, finding interpreters . . . learned
that these are the initial letters of names, the first of
Christ and the second of Konstantios.

JULIAN, *Misopogon* (The Beard-Hater)

How could they ever give up
their marvelous way of life, the range
of their daily pleasures, their brilliant theatre
which consummated a union between Art
and the erotic proclivities of the flesh?

Immoral to a degree—and probably more than a degree—
they certainly were. But they had the satisfaction of living
the notorious life of Antioch,
delectable, in absolute good taste.

To give up all this, indeed, for what?

His hot air about the false gods,
his boring self-advertisement,
his childish fear of the theatre,
his graceless prudery, his ridiculous beard.

Certainly they preferred C,
certainly they preferred K—a hundred times over.

He'd been sitting in the café since ten-thirty
expecting him to show up any minute.
Midnight went by, and he was still waiting for him.
It was now after one-thirty, and the café was almost
  deserted.
He'd grown tired of reading newspapers
mechanically. Of his three lonely shillings
only one was left: waiting that long,
he'd spent the others on coffees and cognac.
And he'd smoked all his cigarettes.
So much waiting had worn him out.
Because alone like that for so many hours,
he'd begun to have disturbing thoughts
about the irregular life he was living.

But when he saw his friend come in—
weariness, boredom, thought disappeared at once.

His friend brought unexpected news.
He'd won sixty pounds playing cards.

Their good looks, their exquisite youthfulness,
the sensitive love they shared
were refreshed, livened, invigorated
by the sixty pounds from the card table.

Now all joy and vitality, feeling and charm,
they went—not to the homes of their respectable families
(where they were no longer wanted anyway)—
they went to a familiar and very special
house of debauchery, and they asked for a bedroom
and expensive drinks, and they drank again.

And when the drinks were finished
and it was close to four in the morning,
happy, they gave themselves to love.

Brain, work now as well as you can.
A partial pleasure's destroying him.
He's in a maddening situation.
Every day he kisses the face he worships,
his hands are on those magnificent limbs.
He's never loved before with this degree of passion.
But the rich fulfillment of love
is lacking: that fulfillment
which both of them have to want with the same intensity.

(They aren't equally given to homosexual love;
he alone is completely possessed by it.)

And so he's destroying himself, he's all on edge.
Then—to make things worse—he's out of work.
He manages somehow to borrow
a little here and there (sometimes almost begging for it)
and he just gets by.
He kisses those adored lips, excites himself
on that wonderful body—though he now feels
it only acquiesces. And then
he drinks and smokes, drinks and smokes;
and he drags himself to the cafés all day long,
wearily drags the sickness consuming his beauty.
Brain, work now as well as you can.

He didn't know, King Kleomenis, he didn't dare—
he just didn't know how to tell his mother
a thing like that: Ptolemy's demand,
to guarantee their treaty, that she too go
to Egypt and be held there as a hostage—
a very humiliating, indecorous thing.
And he would be about to speak yet always hesitate,
would start to tell her yet always stop.

But the wonderful woman understood him
(she'd already heard some rumors about it)
and she encouraged him to get it out.
And she laughed, and said of course she'd go,
happy that even in old age
she could be useful to Sparta still.

As for the humiliation—that didn't touch her at all.
Of course an upstart like the Lagid
couldn't possibly comprehend the Spartan spirit;
so his demand couldn't in fact humiliate
an exalted lady like herself:
mother of a Spartan king.

That things in the Colony aren't what they should be
no one can doubt any longer,
and though in spite of everything we do move forward,
maybe—as more than a few believe—the time has come
to bring in a Political Reformer.

But here's the problem, the objection:
they make a tremendous fuss
about everything, these reformers.
(What a relief it would be
if they were never needed.) They probe everywhere,
question the smallest detail,
and right away think up radical reforms
that demand immediate execution.

Also, they have a liking for sacrifice:
GET RID OF THAT POSSESSION;
YOUR OWNING IT IS PRECARIOUS:
POSSESSIONS LIKE THOSE ARE WHAT RUIN COLONIES.
GET RID OF THAT INCOME,
AND THE OTHER CONNECTED WITH IT,
AND THIS THIRD, AS A NATURAL CONSEQUENCE:
THEY ARE SUBSTANTIAL, BUT WHAT CAN ONE DO?
THE RESPONSIBILITY THEY CREATE IS DAMAGING.

And as they extend the range of their control
they find an endless number of useless things to eliminate—
things which are, however, difficult to give up.

And when, all being well, they finish the job,
every detail now diagnosed and sliced away,
and they retire (also taking the wages due to them),
it's a wonder anything's left at all
after such surgical efficiency.

Maybe the moment hasn't arrived yet.
Let's not be too hasty: speed is a dangerous thing.
Untimely measures bring repentance.
Certainly, and unhappily, many things are wrong in the
     Colony.
But is there anything human without some fault?
And after all, you see, we do move forward.

Aristomenis, son of Menelaos,
the Prince from Western Libya,
was generally liked in Alexandria
during the ten days he spent there.
In keeping with his name, his dress was also properly
    Greek.
He received honors gladly,
but he didn't solicit them; he was unassuming.
He bought Greek books,
especially history and philosophy.
Above all he spoke very little.
Word spread that he must be a profound thinker,
and men like that naturally don't speak very much.

He wasn't a profound thinker or anything at all—
just a piddling, laughable man.
He assumed a Greek name, dressed like the Greeks,
learned to behave more or less like a Greek;
and all the time he was terrified he'd spoil
his reasonably good image
by coming out with barbaric howlers in Greek
and the Alexandrians, bastards that they are,
would start in their normal way to make fun of him.

This was why he limited himself to a few words,
terribly careful of his syntax and pronunciation;
and he almost went out of his mind, having
so much talk bottled up inside him.

When I heard the terrible news, that Myris was dead,
I went to his house, although I avoid
going to the houses of Christians,
especially during times of mourning or festivity.

I stood in the corridor. I didn't want
to go further inside because I saw
that the relatives of the deceased looked at me
with evident surprise and displeasure.

They had him in a large room
and from the corner where I stood
I could catch a glimpse of it: all precious carpets,
and vessels of silver and gold.

I stood and wept in a corner of the corridor.
And I thought how our gatherings and excursions
wouldn't be worthwhile now without Myris;
and I thought how I'd no longer see him
at our wonderfully indecent night-long sessions
enjoying himself, laughing, and reciting verses
with his perfect feel for Greek rhythm;
and I thought how I'd lost forever
his beauty, lost forever
the young man I'd worshipped so passionately.

Some old women close to me were talking with lowered
    voices
about the last day he lived:
the name of Christ constantly on his lips,
his hand holding a cross.
Then four Christian priests
came into the room, and said prayers
fervently, and orisons to Jesus,
or to Mary (I'm not very familiar with their religion).

We'd known of course that Myris was a Christian.
We'd known it from the start,
when he first joined us the year before last.
But he lived exactly as we did:
more given to pleasure than all of us,
he scattered his money lavishly on his amusements.
Not caring a damn what people thought,
he threw himself eagerly into night-time scuffles
when we happend to clash
with some rival group in the street.
He never spoke about his religion.
And once we even told him
that we'd take him with us to the Serapion.
But—I remember now—
he didn't seem to like this joke of ours.
And yes, now I recall two other incidents.
When we made libations to Poseidon,
he drew himself back from our circle and looked elsewhere.
And when one of us in his fervor said:
"May all of us be favored and protected
by the great, the sublime Apollo"—Myris whispered
(the others didn't hear), "not counting me."

The Christian priests were praying loudly
for the young man's soul.
I noticed with how much diligence,
how much intense concern
for the forms of their religion, they were preparing
everything for the Christian funeral.
And suddenly an odd sensation
came over me. Indefinably I felt
as if Myris were going from me:

I felt that he, a Christian, was united
with his own people and that I was becoming
a stranger, a total stranger. I even felt
a doubt assailing me: that I'd been deceived by my passion
and had always been a stranger to him.
I rushed out of their horrible house,
rushed away before my memory of Myris
could be captured, could be perverted by their Christianity.

Thoroughly satisfied by their success,
King Alexander Jannaios
and his wife Queen Alexandra
move through the streets of Jerusalem
with musicians in the lead
and every kind of pomp and circumstance.
The work begun by the great Judas Maccabaios
and his four celebrated brothers
has now been brilliantly fulfilled—
work carried on relentlessly
among so many obstacles and dangers.
Nothing unseemly remained now.
All subservience to the haughty monarchs
of Antioch was over: clearly
King Alexander Jannaios
and his wife Queen Alexandra
are equal to the Selefkids in every way.
Good Jews, pure Jews, devoted Jews above all.
But when circumstances require,
skilled in speaking Greek,
even on familiar terms with Greeks and Hellenized
    monarchs—
as equals, though, let that be clear.
The work begun by the great Judas Maccabaios
and his four celebrated brothers
has been brilliantly fulfilled,
indeed remarkably fulfilled.

Kratisiklia didn't allow
the people to see her weeping and grieving:
she walked in dignified silence.
Her sorrow, her agony,
weren't visible at all on her calm face.
But even so, for a moment she couldn't hold back:
before she went aboard the detestable ship for Alexandria
she took her son to Poseidon's temple,
and when they were there alone
(he was "in deep pain," says Plutarch, "and badly shaken")
she embraced him and kissed him.
But then her strong character struggled through;
and regaining her poise, the magnificent woman
said to Kleomenis: "Come, O King of the Lacedaimonians,
when we go out from here
let no one see us
weeping or doing anything unworthy of Sparta.
This alone is in our power;
our fate will be whatever the god grants."

And she boarded the ship, going toward "whatever the
    god grants."

He left the office where he'd been given
a trivial, poorly paid job
(something like eight pounds a month, including extras)—
left the desolate work
that kept him bent all afternoon,
emerged at seven and walked off slowly,
idling his way down the street.—Good-looking;
and interesting: from the way he showed that he'd reached
the full capacity of his senses.
He'd turned twenty-nine the month before.

He idled his way down the main street
and the poor side-streets that led to his home.

Passing in front of a small shop
where they sold workers
fake merchandise cheaply,
he saw a face inside, a figure
that compelled him to go in, and he pretended
he wanted to look at some colored handkerchiefs.

He asked about the quality of the handkerchiefs
and how much they cost, his voice choking,
almost silenced by desire.
And the answers came back in the same mood,
distracted, the voice hushed,
offering hidden consent.

They kept on talking about the merchandise—
but the only purpose: that their hands might touch
over the handkerchiefs, that their faces, their lips,
might move close together—
a moment's meeting of limb against limb.

Quickly, secretly, so the shop owner sitting at the back
wouldn't realize what was going on.

I'm just about broke and out in the street.
This fatal city, Antioch,
has swallowed all my money:
this fatal city with its extravagant life.

But I'm young and extremely healthy.
Prodigious master of Greek,
I know Aristotle and Plato through and through
as well as the poets and orators or anyone else you could
    mention.
I have a fair idea about military matters
and friends among the senior mercenaries.
I also have a foot in the administrative world;
I spent six months in Alexandria last year:
I know (and this is useful) something about what goes on
    there—
the corrupt scheming, the dirty deals, and the rest of it.

So I believe I'm completely qualified
to serve this country,
my beloved fatherland, Syria.

Whatever the job they give me,
I'll try to be useful to the country. That's what I want.
But if they frustrate me with their maneuvers—
we know them, those smart operators: no need to mention
    them here—
if they frustrate me, it's not my fault.

I'll approach Zabinas first,
and if that idiot doesn't appreciate me,
I'll go to his rival, Grypos.
And if that imbecile doesn't appoint me,
I'll immediately go to Hyrkanos.

One of the three will want me anyway.

And my conscience is quiet
about my not caring which one I choose:
the three of them are equally bad for Syria.

But, a ruined man, it's not my fault.
I'm only trying, poor devil, to make ends meet.
The almighty gods ought to have taken the trouble
to create a fourth, an honest man.
I would have gladly gone along with him.

"Alexander, son of Philip, and the Greeks except the Lace-
daimonians. . . ."

We can well imagine
how utterly indifferent the Spartans would have been
to this inscription. "Except the Lacedaimonians"—
that goes without saying. The Spartans weren't to be led
and ordered about
like precious servants. Besides,
they wouldn't have thought a pan-Hellenic expedition
without a Spartan king in command
was to be taken very seriously.
Of course, then, "except the Lacedaimonians."

That's certainly a way of looking at it. Quite
    understandable.

So, except the Lacedaimonians at Granicos;
and then at Issus; then in the decisive battle
where the terrible army
the Persians mustered at Arbela was routed:
it set out for victory from Arbela, and was routed.

And from this amazing pan-Hellenic expedition,
triumphant, brilliant in every way,
celebrated on all sides, glorified
as no other has ever been glorified,
incomparable, we emerged:
the great new Hellenic world.

We the Alexandrians, the Antiochians,
the Selefkians, and the countless
other Greeks of Egypt and Syria,
and those in Midia, and Persia, and all the rest:
with our far-flung supremacy,
our flexible policy of judicious integration,
and our communal Greek language
which we carried into Bactria, even to the Indians.

Who gives a damn about the Lacedaimonians now!

We were astonished in Antioch when we heard
what Julian was up to now.

Apollo had made things clear to him at Daphni!
He didn't want to give an oracle (as though we cared!),
he didn't intend to speak prophetically, unless
his temple at Daphni was purified first.
The nearby dead, he declared, made him uneasy.

There are many tombs at Daphni.
One of the people buried there
was the triumphant martyr Vavylas,
wonder and glory of our church.

It was him the false god hinted at, him he feared.
As long as he felt him near he didn't dare
pronounce his oracle: not a murmur.
(The false gods are terrified of our martyrs.)

The unholy Julian rolled up his sleeves,
grew wild and shouted: "Raise him, carry him out,
take him away immediately, this Vavylas.
You there, do you hear? Apollo is uneasy.
Grab him, raise him at once,
dig him out, take him wherever you want,
take him away, throw him out. I'm not just playing around.
Apollo said the temple has to be purified."

We took it, the holy relic, and carried it elsewhere.
We took it, we carried it in love and in honor.

And hasn't the temple prospered wonderfully since!
In no time at all a colossal fire broke out,
a terrible fire,
and both the temple and Apollo burned to the ground.

Ashes the idol: trash to be swept away.

Julian blew up, and he spread word—
what else could he do?—that we, the Christians,
had set the fire. Let him say so.
It hasn't been proved. Let him say so.
The crucial thing is: he blew up.

Notes

3. CHE FECE . . . IL GRAN RIFIUTO [WHO MADE . . . THE GREAT REFUSAL]. *Inferno*, III, 60. The complete phrase (ll. 59-60) reads: "colui che fece per viltate il gran rifiuto." The man who "refused" is generally assumed to be Celestine V. He was elected Pope in 1294 and gave up his office after five months in order to return to monastic life.

4. THERMOPYLAE. Ephialtis was the Malian Greek who treacherously guided a section of the Persian army over a mountain path in order to attack the rear of the Greek forces, under Leonidas, which were then protecting the pass of Thermopylae (480 B.C.).

11. THE FOOTSTEPS. The Lares were minor Roman deities who protected the household, in this case that of Nero's family, the Aenobarbi.

13. THE SATRAPY. A satrapy was a province governed by a Satrap under the ancient Persian monarchy. The protagonist of the poem is someone like Dimaratos (see the poem of that title, p. 54): a Greek who took refuge in the Persian court.

14. THE IDES OF MARCH. Artemidoros, a friend of Julius Caesar, taught the Greek language in Rome. (Cf. Shakespeare, *Julius Caesar*, II, iii, and III, i.)

16. THE GOD ABANDONS ANTONY. Cf. Shakespeare, *Antony and Cleopatra*, IV, iii.

20. PHILHELLENE. The speaker is presumably a Selefkid monarch. Zagros was the range of mountains dividing Midia from Assyria and Susiana in Asia Minor. Phraata was a great city of Midia, winter home of the Parthian kings.

26. EXILES. Nonnos (fl. c. A.D. 400) was a Greek epic poet, born in Panopolis, Egypt. Basil is the Byzantine Emperor Basil I (867-886), who came to the throne after murdering his coemperor, Michael III. Basil wasn't in fact overthrown; he reigned for close to twenty years, until his death from old age. The exiles of this poem may well have been

friends of the Patriarch of Constantinople, Photius, who was deposed by Basil early in his reign.

27. THEODOTOS. Plutarch, in his *Life of Pompey*, says that Theodotos of Chios persuaded the Egyptians to kill Pompey when he landed in Egypt after the battle of Pharsalia. Pompey's head was brought to Caesar when he reached Egypt shortly after the murder.

30. OROPHERNIS. Dimitrios Sotir, one of the grandsons of Antiochos the Great, was King of Syria from 162-150 B.C. (See "Of Dimitrios Sotir," p. 45.)

32. THE BATTLE OF MAGNESIA. The protagonist of this poem is Philip V, King of Macedonia (220-178 B.C.), who was defeated by the Romans under the consul Flamininus at the battle of Cynoscephalae in 197 B.C., that is, seven years before Antiochos the Great, King of Syria (223-187 B.C.), was also defeated by the Romans under Scipio Africanus Major at the battle of Magnesia.

33. MANUEL KOMNINOS. Manuel Komninos was Byzantine Emperor from 1143 to 1180.

34. THE DISTRESS OF SELEFKIDIS. Dimitrios Selefkidis is the Dimitrios Sotir mentioned in the note to the poem "Orophernis" (p. 30). The Ptolemy of the poem is Ptolemy VI, Philomitor, King of Egypt from 181 to 146 B.C. After being expelled from Alexandria by his brother and coruler, Evergetis, he went to Rome (164 B.C.) to ask the senate to reinstate him. He was successful in his mission.

38. KAISARION. Kaisarion was the son of Julius Caesar and Cleopatra. In 34 B.C. Antony conferred on him the title King of Kings (see the poem "Alexandrian Kings," p. 21), but after Antony's defeat, he was assassinated by Octavius (Augustus) on the advice of his counsellors, who considered Kaisarion a potential rival.

40. NERO'S RESPITE. In the spring of A.D. 68, Galba, then the Roman governor of Spain (Hispania Tarraconensis), was invited by the army to replace Nero; on the latter's suicide in the same year, Galba was proclaimed emperor and went to Rome. Nero's visit to Greece, during which he consulted the oracle, took place a year before this, in A.D. 67.

41. ENVOYS FROM ALEXANDRIA. The "rival Ptolemaic kings" are Ptolemy VI, Philomitor and his brother Evergetis (see the note to "The Distress of Selefkidis," p. 34).

45. OF DIMITRIOS SOTIR (162-150 B.C.). The protagonist of this poem is the Dimitrios Sotir referred to in the poem "Orophernis" (see p. 30). After the defeat of his grandfather, Antiochos the Great, at the battle of Magnesia (see the note to "The Battle of Magnesia," p. 32), Dimitrios Sotir was sent to Rome as a hostage. On the death of Antiochos, he asked to be set free. The senate refused, but he managed to escape secretly. After he returned to Syria, the people declared in his favor, and he finally obtained recognition as king from the Romans. He expelled the satrap Herakleidis from Babylon, thereby earning the title Sotir. But through the excesses of his life he lost his people's support, was overthrown by an impostor, Valas, and was killed by him in battle.

47. IF ACTUALLY DEAD. Apollonius of Tyana (a town in Cappadocia) was born about four years before Christ. After studying Greek philosophy and adopting the ascetic life of a strict Pythagorean, he travelled widely in the East (even visiting India) and became famous for his miraculous powers. The last years of his life were spent at Ephesus. Many of his wonders, which are related by his biographer, Philostratos (b. A.D. 182), have clear similarities to the miracles of Christ. Philostratos' biography was allegedly based on the memoirs of a certain Damis, a native of Ninevah, who is mentioned in the poem as a source. The pagan who "muses" in the poem lived in the reign of the Byzantine Emperor, Justin I (A.D. 518-527).

48. YOUNG MEN OF SIDON (A.D. 400). The complete epitaph on Aeschylus reads as follows: "In this tomb lies Aeschylus, son of Euphorion, an Athenian, who died in wheat-bearing Gela. The Marathonian grove may proclaim his renowned valor, and the long-haired Medes, who knew it well." There is some question as to whether Aeschylus himself composed the epitaph; in any case—as the young Sidonian contends—it says nothing about Aeschylus' creative work and merely commemorates the fact that the tragedian fought

against the Persians at Marathon, where (in 480 B.C.) the Greeks defeated the army of Dareios, which was led by Datis and Artaphernis.

49. DAREIOS. Dareios was king from 521 to 485 B.C. Mithridatis VI (called Evpator, Dionysos, and the Great) was King of Pontos from 120 to 63 B.C. Cicero designated him the greatest of all kings after Alexander and the most formidable opponent that the Roman army of his day encountered. Amisos, one of Mithridatis' residences, was a large city on the coast of Pontos.

51. ANNA KOMNINA. Anna Komnina (1083-1146) was the daughter of the Byzantine Emperor Alexios I Komninos (1081-1118), and her *Alexiad* was a biography of her father. "Impudent John" refers to her brother, John II, who succeeded their father as Emperor and ruled for 25 years, successfully forestalling his sister's attempt to obtain the throne for her husband so that she could be his Empress.

52. AN EXILED BYZANTINE NOBLEMAN WHO COMPOSES VERSES. Botaniatis is the Byzantine Emperor Nikiforos III (1078-1081), who was dethroned by Alexios I Komninos (see the above note), husband of Irini Doukaina.

53. ALEXANDER VALAS. Valas is the impostor mentioned in the note on "Of Dimitrios Sotir," p. 45.

54. DIMARATOS. Dimaratos was King of Sparta from about 510 to 491 B.C. After his colleague, Kleomenis (aided by Leotychidis), unscrupulously bribed the Delphic oracle in order to establish that Dimaratos was an illegitimate son of Ariston, Dimaratos retreated to the Persian court of Dareios, where he was well received. He subsequently accompanied Xerxes on his unsuccessful campaign against the Greeks.

56. FROM THE SCHOOL OF THE RENOWNED PHILOSOPHER. The "renowned philosopher" is Ammonios (d. A.D. 243; "Sakkas" because as a porter he once carried sacks of wheat). He taught in Alexandria and is said to have had Longinus, Herennius, Plotinus, and Origen among his disciples.

57. JULIAN SEEING CONTEMPT. Julian the Apostate was Roman Emperor from A.D. 361 to 363. He tried unsuccessfully to bring back the strict worship of pagan deities in place of

Christianity. The quotation in the poem is from a letter of his appointing Theodoros High Priest throughout Asia.

58. EPITAPH OF ANTIOCHOS, KING OF KOMMAGINI. The Antiochos of this poem is possibly Antiochos I (c. 69-31 B.C.) of Kommagini, a small state that was originally a part of the Greek kingdom of Syria. The epitaph is Cavafy's construction.

59. IN ALEXANDRIA, 31 B.C. The incident in this poem is set at the time of Antony's final defeat by Octavius at the sea-battle of Actium, off western Greece.

60. JOHN KANTAKUZINOS TRIUMPHS. The unnamed protagonist lived in the middle of the fourteenth century. When the Byzantine Emperor Andronikos III Palaiologos died (1341), John Kantakuzinos was appointed Regent. This initiated a struggle for power between him and the widow of Andronikos III, Anna of Savoy, mother of the eleven-year-old successor to the throne, John V. In 1347, Kantakuzinos "triumphed" in this struggle and was crowned joint Emperor as John VI, his wife, Irini Asan, then becoming Empress.

61. OF COLORED GLASS. The royal protagonists of this poem are those mentioned in the above note. Vlachernai was a church in Constantinople.

64. IN A TOWNSHIP OF ASIA MINOR. See the note to "In Alexandria, 31 B.C.," p. 59.

65. A GREAT PROCESSION OF PRIESTS AND LAYMEN: See the note to "Julian Seeing Contempt," p. 57. In 363, Julian was killed in battle while fighting against the Persians, and Jovian, a Christian, was proclaimed his successor.

66. JULIAN AND THE ANTIOCHIANS. The quotation heading this poem is from a satirical work by Julian (see the note to "Julian Seeing Contempt," p. 57) in which he attacks the people of Antioch, then a Christian city, for their hostile attitude toward his attempts to restore his prudish and moralistic form of paganism. The poem expresses the response of the Antiochians to Julian's pedantic attack.

69. IN SPARTA. Kleomenis (King of Sparta from 236 to 222 B.C.) had agreed to send his mother, Kratisiklia, and his children as hostages to Egypt on the condition that Ptolemy III Evergetis, King of Egypt, would send him aid in his war

against Macedonia and the Achaian League. Lagid means son
of Lagos, or, here, Ptolemy III.

76. ALEXANDER JANNAIOS AND ALEXANDRA. Alexander
Jannaios was King of the Jews from 104 to 77 B.C. He reached
the throne after what John Mavrogordato calls "judicious mas-
sacres" (*The Poems of C. P. Cavafy*, London, 1952, p. 183),
and thus completed the "Hellenizing" policy of the Maccabees,
which itself ended in further bloodshed.

77. COME, O KING OF THE LACEDAIMONIANS. See the note
to "In Sparta," p. 69.

79. TO HAVE TAKEN THE TROUBLE. Zabinas, Grypos, and
Hyrkanos had direct political interests in Syria during the
second century B.C., the first two as rivals for the Syrian throne
and the third as King of the Jews.

81. IN THE YEAR 200 B.C. The opening line of the poem
is from an inscription which Alexander the Great wrote to
accompany the booty he sent to Athens from his conquests in
Persia. It emphasizes the fact that the Spartans refused to
participate in this "amazing pan-Hellenic expedition." The
significance of the date in the title (200 B.C.) is that the
speaker in the poem is quoting the inscription some 130 years
after Alexander's victories and three years before the battle
of Cynoscephalae, when Philip V (see the note to "The Battle
of Magnesia," p. 32), the last of the Macedonian Philips, was
crushingly defeated by the Romans. It is also ten years before
the defeat of Antiochos the Great at the battle of Magnesia (see
the same note), which marked the Roman conquest of "the
great new Hellenic world" mentioned in the poem.

83. ON THE OUTSKIRTS OF ANTIOCH. See the notes to
"Julian Seeing Contempt," p. 57, and "Julian and the Antioch-
ians," p. 66.

Biographical Note

CONSTANTINE P. CAVAFY (Kavafis), born in Alexandria, Egypt, in 1863, was the ninth and last child of Constantinopolitan parents. His father, Peter, was descended from a line of Phanariots going back at least to 1700; and his mother, Hariklia, also came from a family long established in Constantinople. Peter Cavafy moved to Alexandria in 1850, but some years before settling there, he helped organize the Alexandrian Greek community; and after taking up residence, he became vice-president of the community council (1854-1857). With his brother George—then living in England—he also founded Cavafy and Company, an export-import firm that prospered for some years dealing in Egyptian cotton and Manchester textiles. During the Crimean War he relinquished his Greek citizenship in order to come under British protection, thus opening the way for what proved a long and significant association between Cavafy and England. In 1872, two years after her husband's death, Hariklia moved her family to Liverpool; and when the assets of Cavafy and Company were liquidated by her brother-in-law during the Egyptian financial crisis of 1876, she decided to remain in England for another three years to collect her husband's share. Before returning to Alexandria in 1879, she solicited and obtained British passports for herself and three of her sons, including Constantine.

The seven years that Cavafy spent in England, between the ages of nine and sixteen, were important in the shaping of his poetic sensibility. Apart from his reading in English literature, he became so much at home in the English language and so familiar with English manners that the influence of both remained with him throughout his life (he is reported to have spoken his native Greek with a slight British accent until the day he died). His first verse was written in English (signed "Constantine Cavafy"), and both his subsequent practice as a poet and his limited prose criticism demonstrate a substantial familiarity with the English poetic tradition, in particular the works of Shakespeare, Browning, and Oscar Wilde.

Immediately after Cavafy returned to Alexandria from London, he enrolled for a brief period at the Hermis Lyceum, a commercial school that served the leading families in the Greek community. This is the only instance of formal education indicated by the biographical data currently available to us. During the same period he began a historical dictionary that was interrupted significantly at the entry "Alexander." Then, in 1882, before the British bombardment of Alexandria (which ultimately damaged Cavafy's home), Hariklia again moved her family abroad for a three-year interval, this time back to Constantinople. It proved to be another significant stage in the development of Cavafy's sensibility. He wrote his first poems—in English, French, and Greek—during this interval, and he apparently had his first homosexual love affair. There is also some evidence that he began to think of a career in politics or journalism; and soon after his return to Alexandria in 1885, he received a press card as correspondent for the Alexandrian newspaper *Telegraphos*. He also recovered his Greek nationality. But his ambition during the years that followed was in fact devoted almost entirely to the writing of poems and a few prose essays, including one in English entitled "Give Back the Elgin Marbles."

At the age of twenty-nine Cavafy took up an appointment as special clerk in the Irrigation Service of the Ministry of Public Works, a position that he held for the next thirty years and that provided the principal source of his income, supplemented by speculative earnings (sometimes quite substantial) on the Egyptian Stock Exchange, which admitted him as a broker in 1894. His Greek citizenship precluded his becoming a member of the so-called "permanent staff" of the Service, which was restricted to British or Egyptian subjects, but during the course of his career he received regular increases in salary (from £7 a month in 1892 to £33 a month in 1919), and he retired in 1922 with the rank of "Assistant Director." He continued to live in Alexandria until his death, from cancer of the larynx, in 1933. It is recorded that he received the holy communion of the Orthodox Church shortly before dying, and that his last motion was to draw a circle on a blank sheet of paper and then place a period in the middle of the circle.

From the outline of this sparse history, it would seem that Cavafy's richest life had to be the inner life sustained by his personal relations and his artistic creativity. Yet what little is known of the poet's social life suggests an image that is equally undramatic. There is now some reason to question the traditional view of Cavafy as an isolated figure hiding behind the dim candlelight of a stuffy, book-lined room (Sareyiannis' memoir indicates that the poet received visitors often and was known to be a stimulating, loquacious host when the mood struck him). At the same time, the bare facts of his biography suggest an unusually restricted circle of personal relations. He lived with his mother until her death in 1899, then with his unmarried brothers, and for most of his mature years, alone. The poet himself identified only two love affairs, both apparently transitory (see the comment on "September, 1903" and "December, 1903" in *C. P. Cavafy: Passions and Ancient Days*, New York, 1971, p. 63). A diary—largely unpublished—reveals that Cavafy was tormented until his middle forties not by complications resulting from homosexual relationships (as a number of his erotic poems might lead one to think) but by guilt over what he felt to be a relentless autoeroticism. His one intimate, long-standing friendship, so far as is known, was with Alexander Singopoulos, whom Cavafy designated his heir and literary executor some ten years before his death, that is, when the poet was sixty years old.

Cavafy did maintain several influential literary relationships during his later years, including a twenty-year acquaintance with E. M. Forster; and as his unique contribution to twentieth-century poetry began to receive some local recognition, he became one of the few literary personalities European visitors to Alexandria might try to approach. Several of those who managed to search him out have reported that Cavafy was not only a receptive host but a learned conversationalist who had the fascinating capacity to gossip about historical figures from the distant past so as to make them seem a part of some scandalous intrigue taking place in the Alexandrian world immediately below the poet's second-floor balcony. Yet for all his local renown, Cavafy remained virtually unrecognized in Greece until late in his career (an article on his poetry by Grigori Xenopoulos in 1903 is a revealing exception), and his own attitude toward the public presentation of his work suggested an "uncommon esthetic asceticism" (as expressed in the introduction to *Passions and Ancient Days*). Cavafy never offered a volume of his poems for sale during his lifetime; his method of distributing his work was to give friends and relatives the several pamphlets of his poems that he had printed privately and a folder of his latest broadsheets or offprints held together by a large clip. The only evidence of some public recognition in Greece during his later years was his receipt, in 1926, of the Order of the Phoenix from the Greek dictator Pangalos, and his appointment, in 1930, to the International Committee for the Rupert Brooke memorial statue that was placed on the island of Skyros. The latter may have been partly a consequence of the recognition Cavafy had gained in England by that time, including publication of "Ithaka" in T. S. Eliot's *Criterion* and the enthusiastic interest of T. E. Lawrence, Arnold Toynbee, and others who had been introduced to his work by E. M. Forster.

Though Cavafy met various men of letters during his several trips to Athens (including a four-month visit for medical reasons shortly before his death), he did not receive his full measure of appreciation from the Athenian literati until some time after the publication of his first collected edition in 1935. It seems likely that his importance went relatively unrecognized before his death for exactly those reasons that have now established him as perhaps the most original and influential Greek poet of this century: his uncompromising distaste, in his mature years, for rhetoric of the kind then prevalent among his contemporary poets in mainland Greece; his almost prosaic frugality in the use of figures and metaphors; his constant evocation of spoken rhythms and colloquialisms; his frank, avant-garde treatment of homosexual themes; his reintroduction of epigrammatic and dramatic modes that had remained largely dormant since Hellenistic times; his often esoteric but brilliantly alive sense of history; his commitment to Hellenism, coupled with an astute cynicism about politics; his aesthetic perfectionism. These characteristics, not yet in fashion during his day, and his refusal to enter the market place even to buy prestige, may have prevented him from realizing all but the most private rewards for his genius. They are also among the characteristics most likely to assure him an enduring place in the longest literary tradition the Western world has known.

E.K.